What are
Life, Death, and Wonder:
Twenty Years with a Pack of Dogs?

<u>Life, Death, and Wonder: Twenty Years with a Pack of Dogs</u> *is a wonderful book of poems and reflective essays. Penthea Burns brings us behind her dog's eyes of liquid compassion, wisdom, patience, and love in a unique way: the dog becomes 'teacher'... the conduit for our God-given omniscient inner source of knowledge. They too become the mirror through which we see and reflect our own soul's beauty, and in an honest, heartwarming, deeper way, through which Penthea powerfully allows us into her relationship with God. Through her interchange of love of her 'pack' and her inner reflection, it is impossible to not see the beauty within each one of us. This is a book about joy and healing, and finding strength in the purity and grace of unconditional love, both given and received.*
～ Claire Hersom, poet, organizer of The Bookey Readings at the Harlow Gallery, author of *Drowning: A Poetic Memoir*, *The Day I Circled The Wagons*, and *Supper at The Farm*

The poems in Penthea Burns' <u>Life, Death, and Wonder: Twenty Years with a Pack of Dogs</u> *are vivid with stunning scenes of nature and gratitude for meaning found in everyday life. These poems show us the gifts that come when we love with an open heart, how when we care for others we become healed ourselves, how the earth is one of our best teachers and how all life speaks a language that can be heard when we slow down and listen. The dogs in these poems are faithful guardians in this world and the next. Burns has a gift for humanizing the earth, dogs and the underrepresented people, bringing all she is connected with into her team.*
～ Lisa Panepinto, poet and author of *This Borrowed Bike*

I'm a dog. People might not expect that a dog, like me, would have much to say, let alone believe that I would collaborate to write poetry. Love has a way of inspiring hearts and stretching us beyond what we think of as our capacity. Dogs and trees and songbirds and dolphins all know this (god, I hope to meet a dolphin). All of creation speaks. Anyone who listens with their heart knows this. Penthea listens and writes it down. That's where this collection of poems came from. It's all about the love. And I love my blue collar.
    ~ GreatMountain Tupelo Jackman, Chinook dog

From the softball fields and journals of her youth to the organizations and myriad grants of her career, Penthea has always been a team player and a writer. Ironically, it was the routines and chaos of sharing her home with Chinooks that inspired her to initiate the slow, solitary exploration into her poetic voice. Penthea writes the way she lives - with a lavishly generous and tender heart.
    ~ Rebecca Johanna Stephans, teacher, friend, animal lover

A benediction and a challenge, <u>Life, Death and Wonder: Twenty Years with a Pack of Dogs</u>, *enfolds you in the winsome peace of Penthea's connection to her beloved dogs and life around her. It challenges you to be open and vulnerable, to renounce the easy cynicism keeping pace with the flow of modern life, so that you, too, can learn what it is to honestly feel for a moment, an interaction, a lifetime.*
    ~ Karen Hinchy, Chinook owner/breeder, President of the Chinook Owners Association

Life, Death, and Wonder

*Twenty Years with a
Pack of Dogs*

Penthea Burns

GreatMountain Farm Press
Lewiston, ME

Copyright © 2017 by Penthea Burns

All rights reserved. This book or any portion thereof may not be reproduced or used in any manner whatsoever without the express written permission of the publisher except for the use of brief quotations in a book review or scholarly journal.

First Printing: 2017

ISBN 978-1-365-73358-1

GreatMountain Farm
PO Box 2334
Lewiston, ME 04241

Dedication

To the dogs of my life –

Smokey, Lobo, Smackwater Jack, Gretchen Barker, Katahdin Wind, Rangeley Runner, Baxter Boulevard, Cheena, Tangles, North Trav'ler, Allagash Springs, Nokomis Dream, Ripley, Baring, Moxie, Chocorua Moon, Otter, Yukon Charley, Mahoosuc, Tupelo Jackman, Redington Guide, Strider, Dirigo, and countless puppies.

From you, I learned to pay attention to life's daily and simple abundance – a walk, a good belly rub, food, singing, napping. Because of you, I aspire to be in this moment. With you, I learned about getting out of my head's brain and living more in the brain that fills my heart, my gut, my body – go outside, run, get my hands in the dirt, and put my feet on the ground.

And love – unconditional love. Thank you for giving and receiving.

Thank you for greeting me with unbridled joy each time I returned home.

Thank you for trusting me.

Thank you for introducing me to some of my favorite people.

A special note to Gretchen Barker, thank you for saving my life.

With love
Penthea

Acknowledgements

Mary Burns (Mom)
To my Mom, Mary Burns, who encouraged my love of poetry for as long as I can remember. Thank you for that gift, among many others. I love you.

Jess Maurer
It all started with walking Gubby (Gretchen) around the neighborhood and a few conversations with our nice neighbors...who had A LOT of dogs.

And then there was this little puppy with a white blaze on her face – Katahdin – who came home with us one day. A lot more happened after that. In the end, we were blessed with loving and being loved by the dogs listed in this book's dedication – while we lived together and today as we live in separate homes.

I learned a lot about dogs and myself in the process. I'm glad to share this experience with you.

Braden Maurer-Burns
Thank you for taking a chance on us when you really were more of a cat person. There would be a big, gaping hole if my life had proceeded without you. I love you.

Chinook Community
I am grateful for the people who I love and admire within the Chinook community – friends who opened their homes and hearts to Chinooks and Chinook people who became friends. We have stories to tell – that will make you laugh, cry, and believe in something more wondrous than our solitary human existence.

My Editorial Team
Pat beautifully edited my first publication, <u>My Prognosis: I Live</u>, published in 2014. Some years before that, she challenged me to write a poem a day. That simple act stimulated a different discipline and attention to writing for which I am grateful.

My deep gratitude goes to Julie Atkins who, through tears, graciously edited this edition of poems.

Rebecca who found grammatical errors and missing or extra spaces. She edited with attention to my voice and intention and with love of these words.

Many thanks to Angie Bordeaux for the final steps of formatting (page numbering and section breaks vexed me) and getting the cover just right from a technical and creative perspective – two or three times! Life saver!

NVC
Peggy, Leah, Rebecca and my dear practice buddies. The language and learning from NVC has intensified self-understanding and fostered more satisfying connections in my life. It has strengthened my presence with and observation of the world around me and inside of me. Writing has been more deeply satisfying as a result.

Table of Contents

Preface	1

Poetry & Essay Contents

Conversations, Inspirations, and Gifts

What I Learned in My Life with Dogs	7
Who You Love More	11
Tell Me a Secret	12
Dog Conversation # 23	14
This is a Poem about Red	15
Tell Me A Story	16
Autumn Reverence	18
Spirit Dogs	19
For An Old Dog	20
Gifts	22

Dogs, Me, and the World

Faith – Magical Thinking – Belief in Magic	27
The Heart Finds Its Healing	29
A Trav'ler's Vow	31
My Father	32
Dog Naps and Dreams	34
For Not Mowing	36
Home	37
Morning Meditation with Dogs	38
My Teachers	39
A Blank Page	40
Mother Remembering	41
1:30 AM	42
There It Is	44

Life, Death, and Wonder
But Today   49
Tied to Generations   50
Life, Death, and Wonder with a Pack of Dogs   51
Haikus   55
Solstice Birth   56
Old Dog   57
My Favorite Dreams   58
Trav'ler on a Rainy Spring Day   60
The Story   61
For Trav'ler Who Lives On   62
What is Born?   64
Fly Free (For Ande)   66
Who Will Be the Alpha Dog?   67
Sunday Walk in the Woods   70
First Fire   72
Celebration   73

About the Author   75

More Poetry by Penthea Burns   76

Preface

In 1995 I came out of the closet and began two long-term relationships in quick succession. The first was with a lawyer and political activist named Jess. She was smart, strong-willed, and one of the most generous people I know. Soon after we moved in together, Jess and I began a routine of walking our neighborhood each evening. It began innocently enough – meeting neighbors who also happened to be dog breeders. We met, and within weeks we both were swept off our feet by, a Chinook puppy who we named Katahdin.

Chinooks are a rare breed of sled dog, born in New Hampshire in 1917. After achieving some notoriety by bringing dogsledding to New England, serving in Admiral Byrd's expedition to Antarctica, being named by President Hoover as America's most typical dog, and sledding from Kittery to Fort Kent, Maine, Chinooks slipped into obscurity. While trailblazers in the northeastern U.S., they were outrun on the trail when Siberian Huskies were imported to the States. Moreover, a single person controlled the entire Chinook breeding population, which is simply not sustainable. Since 1981, when Chinooks were on the brink of extinction, an array of people have collaborated and debated with one another to breed litters, address health concerns, implement scientific strategies in response to the tight gene pool, and love these gentle giants, now the New Hampshire state dog. See the Chinook Owners Association for more information about the breed – www.chinook.org.

Chinooks are compared to potato chips. "Bet you can't have just one" is really often true. Jess and I swore that we would have just one; we didn't want to breed a litter; well, two is the perfect number because we don't need a dogsled team; ok, we would do our part by breeding one litter but, we wouldn't undertake the ten year crossbreeding program; and we definitely didn't want to be on the Association's board of directors. Each limitation we set out was a limitation that moved as these dogs moved us.

A year after Katahdin's arrival Rangeley joined us with the hope of producing our first litter of puppies. Then Baxter, Cheena, and Allagash found a home with us as we built a dogsled team. We started a breeding kennel, bred our first litter in 1999 (yes, a crossbred litter). Trav'ler and her brother Cedar were born. We adopted a son (Braden), became part of a larger community, and were off on an adventure. It's now twenty-two years, three homes, many a dogsled run, sixteen years on a dog club board of directors, I don't know how many dog shows or obedience classes, thousands of pounds of dog food and dollars in vet bills, one break up, one restored friendship, eighteen dogs (seventeen of these Chinooks), and more than twenty litters of Chinook puppies later. We've grieved the loss of and buried twelve of these beloved companions when life's natural course has ended or when tragedy unexpectedly struck.

I've observed a lot and learned a thing or two.

I'd like to think I've been a good person to my dogs. And I think that is true. What is at least as true, is that these dogs have been loving, heartfelt, and quirky teachers and companions to me over all these years.

The writing of poetry stills me, quiets me, helps me to pause and see. As a poet, I observe day to day moments and absorb life events. I seek to recognize meaning, connections, themes that help me understand the world around me and the world within me.

This collection includes thirty-six poems and six essays written over a five year period. These writings either feature life experiences with dogs or where dogs serve as some kind of reference in the telling of a tale.

This book is divided into three chapters:

Conversations, Inspirations, and Gifts
These poems and one essay include a series of conversations with dogs and studies on what it's like to live in relationship to them. Being a single person living with a pack, I speak to them and they reply. While their "words" are not in English, I understand them. My dogs fit in my landscape. My home is organized around them, their habits and needs. They contribute to the quality of my life.

Dogs, Me, and the World
These poems and two essays provide examples of dogs as spiritual teachers or soul companions. These are not meant to be examples of anthropomorphizing. They are my experiences. Living in close connection with sentient beings has expanded my worldview. They have been integral in understanding and deepening life relations of all sorts.

Life, Death, and Wonder
This final section of poems and three essay tells stories of living with the life cycle of dogs – anticipating and celebrating their birth, witnessing their interrelationships, caring for them as they age and decline, and accompanying them as they transition from this life to whatever is next. They have their own legacy, most notably everlasting love.

At one point, there were as many as thirteen dogs in my home. Today, I live with three dogs. We continue to be a pack and are one another's teachers, companions, loved ones, and life lines.

May these words offer gifts to you as these experiences and relationships with dogs have been gifts to me.

Conversations, Inspirations, and Gifts

Tell me a secret
I whisper to this
Lanky, brown dog
He kisses my cheek

What I Learned in My Life with Dogs

Say yes.
In 1995, my then partner and I walked our neighborhood each day. Tawny heads and dark brown eyes peered over the top of a fence at us, inviting our attention. We said yes. Over the weeks that followed, their humans, Bob and Connie Jones, with smiles and twinkling eyes, invited us to learn about them and their Chinook dogs. We said yes. They offered us a puppy. We recounted all the reasons for saying no. We said yes. We said yes hundreds of times after that to questions neither of us would have ever imagined.

Do what no one expects you to do and sometimes, leave people speechless.
Tangles, a 9 year old Siberian Husky, came to live with us after she retired from a racing team. She was to teach our Chinooks how to work as a team.

Preparing dinner one evening, with Louis Armstrong and Ella Fitzgerald singing, "They Can't Take That Away From Me," Tangles bounced into the kitchen. She looked around as if she were hearing someone she knew. We stood there dumbfounded and watched as she began to sway back and forth, leaning on one foot, then the other. In unison with Satchmo, Tangles reared her head back, closed her eyes, and sang "woo-woo, woo-woo" through the remainder of the song. At the tune's conclusion, she turned and walked out of the kitchen.

Dare to trust.
In the winter of 1997 I came to be known as One Runner Burns.

We set up our dog teams on the road to Crescent Beach, the state park in Cape Elizabeth, Maine. I tingled with the same excitement and nervousness as our barking and howling dogs. We harnessed and hooked Tangles, Rangeley and Katahdin onto the gangline attached to the body of the wooden sled. I stepped off the brake and we traveled over the road and parking lot towards the beach.

My dogs transformed before me - from barking and demanding canines to ethereal athletes. Visible by moonlight and haloed with steam, the only sounds were sled runners on snow and our collective breathing. I crouched low, leaning into the turn and onto the snowy beach. The waves resonated with our breathing as we raced and time stood still. Over the dunes, the trail took us through a field and into the woods. The dim light of the moon grew fainter, silhouettes merged. The dogs never slowed their pace and I was determined to trust them. Out of the darkness a downed beech tree appeared laying across two thirds of the narrow trail. My dog team both dodged and jumped over the tree. I did the same, leaning on the left runner, I lifted the right runner. With the power of trust in my team and intuition we were propelled around and over the tree. One Runner Burns.

Listen to nature.
Puppies often arrive in the middle of the night. Perhaps what gives rise to visionary dreams also initiates the arrival of living beings. Our second litter arrived in April. In the early morning hours, the first puppy's head appeared emerging from the birth canal. He was halfway out with his protective sac already burst open. All we saw was wet and black – head, neck, chest, and forelegs. Pups are blind and deaf at birth and for the first twelve days. They have smell, touch, and taste. This pup, still halfway snuggled inside his mother's warmth reached eagerly and knowingly for the teat and milk that nature had whispered about.

Know your purpose and then live it.
Allagash lived less than three years.

She taught the pack how to sing – muzzles raised toward the moon, one note rising from each dog's belly curling to the sky. She taught them how to sleep with legs and heads and tails draped all over one another – creating some point of physical contact. When Allagash abruptly and mysteriously died, the pack struggled, fought and re-ordered itself. In her life and death, she had taught the pack how to be a pack.

Grieve.
Allagash taught me about full bodied grief.

Drop it.
Yukon Charley loves to eat small animals. Her propensity for hunting has provided me with a series of mental images that I have been unable to erase – a bunny, a snake, a frog, a woodchuck, a rat. I will spare you the image of the rat killing.

Yukon Charley grabbed a chickadee out of mid-air. Its grey tail feathers protruded from the side of her tawny smile.

"Drop it!" was a command too often used with Charley. This time, she opened her mouth. The chickadee just flew away.

Know what you want.
Jack seeks affection by jumping on me wanting physical closeness, his version of doggie hugs. Jack weighs 73 pounds.

In 2011 I was scheduled for a lumpectomy on my left breast within the next two weeks. I wanted to recuperate at home AND I wanted to avoid injury or pain.

An animal communicator spoke with Jackman. She explained to him that his jumping on me would hurt me. She asked him what he was looking for when he jumped on me – "love, love, love" was his response. She negotiated a compromise to which both Jack and I readily agreed. Jack (and I) would get a loving connection and I would be free from injury or pain.

She asked Jack if there was anything else he wanted to say. His reply was, "I love my food and I want a blue collar!"

Love lives on.

I arrived home in the evening after celebrating my 56 birthday. Trav'ler could not rise to greet me and could not remain standing when I helped her up. She was in her 16th year.

As the vet prepared to euthanize Trav'ler, Jess and I lay on the floor on either side of her, spooning. We thanked Trav'ler for her companionship. We told her we loved her and that she was loved by so many. When the Doc administered the injection, Trav'ler kissed Jess, kissed me, rested her chin on the floor and she was gone.

I met a psychic two months after Trav'ler's death. As she walked into the room, she asked if I'd recently lost a dog. She told me that a dog had been running circles around her since she got out of the shower that morning and followed her to our scheduled appointment. She was here. I smiled. On my drive to this appointment, I had asked Trav'ler to please appear.

Trav'ler told the psychic to thank me for helping her to pass on saying, "I had a love sandwich. Who wouldn't want to die like that?"

Who You Love More

Tonight
I turned and looked my dog Jackman
In the eyes
I asked
Who do you love more?
Rattling off a list of
Dear friends and
Beloveds

Jackman blinked
And stared at me
"What do you mean
Love more?"

Ok
I said
You are Jackman
You know how to love
You love them all
I get it
I understand

But what about…

Wait
I thought
No, that's Chocorua

Chocorua
Do you love Nathan Federici more?

Chocorua
Face down in her food dish
Paused
Looked up at me
And walked over wagging…
"Is Nathan here?"

Tell Me a Secret

Jackman, my biggest dog
Climbs onto my lap
Wanting to be the only one
For that moment

Tell me a secret
I whisper to this
Lanky, brown dog
He kisses my cheek
That is common knowledge
I reply
Come on, tell me a secret

"All the world is good"
He begins
"It's just that so many
Do not know this
About themselves
Or the other"
He paused and pondered
His blocky head resting
Atop my heart

Continuing his thoughts
He concluded
"We who know
Carry the burden
To bring this lesson forward"

"When we offer love
Perhaps they will notice
The hunger for love
That lives inside
Perhaps they will recognize
The love they have to give"

Deep brown eyes
Were now looking into my own

"It's all about the love"
Was his final reply

I paused and pondered
My thoughts resting
Within my heart
You are a wise one
I said at last
To Jackman, my biggest dog

"That is common knowledge"
He replied
"Come on, you tell me a secret"

Dog Conversation #23
This morning's conversation

Dogs on my heels
I am going nowhere
I insist
(Disbelief)

Just into the hallway
To get the vacuum
Yes I am going to
Vacuum
And I know you don't
Like the noise
(Stare)

You shed
You run into our house
With muddy paws
"Yes!"

I vacuum
(Blink)

That's our bargain
(Yawn)

This is a Poem about Red

This is a poem about Red
Rather than being a dog she
Wishes to be a hat on my head

Rather than just one of the pack
She prefers the spot on my lap
At the front of the line, all else in the back

Of all of her wishes that bubble and burst
The alpha to all the omegas or better
My one and only not simply the first

Tell Me a Story

I turned to Red
With a variation on a line
That I cleverly deliver
To my dogs –
Tell me a story
I paused to
Listen deeply this time

Red stood close to me
Earnest and wistful
"I have no story
Only urges and sensations
That rise
From deep inside of me
Sometimes it is
Nearly impossible
For me to rest"

I touched her face
Tenderness swelled
And I heard these words
A gift from another
Within me –
All the world is good…
And before another thought travelled
Through my mind
Before even one of those words passed
Through my lips
Red interrupted

"I know this of you
So much has changed
I don't know what I've done
I don't know what I might have done
And the ground beneath me
Is not sure"

I sighed this reply
Ah dear one
What you have done is
Lived and loved
And grieved –
Through the way things are

I cradled Red's soft cheeks
In both my hands
Kissed her forehead
With all the love of the universe

All the world is good
I said
Do you know
That you are good?

I drew back
Looking into her wide eyes
We paused in silence
Movement ceased
We mirrored one another
And rested in presence

Autumn Reverence

Gold and orange
Mountain halo
Dawn greets me
I seek old spirits there
Restless as my own

Gold and red and orange
October trees bejeweled
In celebration
Acknowledgement
Of the passing
Anticipation
Of what is to come
Reverence
For this moment

Gold and red
Buff and tawny
My dogs
My living décor
Hearts offer loyalty
Hearts ask for mine
And for touch

Stories in their brown eyes
Stories in their sighs
Autumn-inspired coats
Rise and fall

Held by their breathing
I linger
In reverence
For this moment

Spirit Dogs

My sled team
Of spirit dogs
Gone beyond
Already one

Indulge my remembrance
Their physical form
My longing to
Bury my face
In their winter coat
Lost in the knowing
Of their deep brown gaze

Lunging
Pulling
Individual and coordinated grace
Raw strength in silence
Whisper the runners against snow

Their breath sends
Misty songs of honor
Living fully
Connected to all beings
Linking all time

For An Old Dog

I groaned – annoyed
When you first woke me
Pulled a pillow over
My head
And hid

I did not sleep again
For I remembered who I am
To you
That your old body
Like mine
Cannot wait long hours

Compassion stirred me
Honoring our agreements – I rose
My companion, my friend

Sleepy, I watched you
Trot out the door
With a grateful roo and
A playful toss of your head

A steady rain is falling now
Trees as silhouettes look black
Against the dark blue morning sky
You sleep soundly
Full belly, head resting
On another dog
I sit in my favorite rocker
Old and low to the ground
My feet propped on the sofa
Where you nap

All I can do
Is bear witness
Take it all in
My senses feast
And I am nourished

I groan with gratitude now
For this
This wonder, this gift
This I could have missed
For thirty minutes more
Of sleep

Gifts

It was oh-dark-thirty
When the first request
To rise sounded
   A whimper
   A bark
   Whimper again

I rise
Bare feet on the cold floor
January morning
The day I was born
A day when I might sleep late

Three dogs dash
Into the front yard
My house faces west
The full moon is low in the sky
Horizon beckons it
   "Come closer
   Sink to my embrace"

My first gift

Dogs safely inside
I retreat to my bed
Dirigo follows
We spoon
   Me under the down comforter
   She atop
Her fur soft, silken
Luxury
Her breath my lullaby
Her small frame against
My aching heart
Not a cure
A faithful companion
To beautiful grief

Of loving and letting go

My second gift

A heavy surrender holds my body now
    Warm and comforted
A familiar *ping* breaks the silence
My smart ass phone – the little distraction
Carries birthday wishes and love
From my favorite angel
Who met me at the airport
Just last night
To deliver pancakes
    For which she is famous
That I might enjoy on this birthday morning

My third gift

Plans to sleep late this morning
Are unfolding a different way
My hands don't wish to stop
Stroking Dirigo's fur
A pancake beckons
My full heart wants more
Of what this day has in store
We rise for real this time
Lingering on the stairs
To greet the sunrise in the east
And Trav'ler who lives in
The early morning light each day
Trav'ler who left earth
On this day two years earlier
Promising me
"You will always remember
Always"

My fourth gift
My fifth gift
And who can count now?

They come so fast
Nestling deeply
Tenderly
In the tenderest
Sturdiest
Parts of me

Dogs, Me, and the World

Jackman sleeps on the sofa
With eyes open
Not for the need of trust
It is for the need of connection

Faith – Magical Thinking – Belief in Magic

Faith provides a framework. It stands on a foundation of principles and beliefs that serve as a reference for my choices, decision-making, and making meaning of life events.

Magical thinking mobilizes when feelings and needs are triggered. It constructs or reconstructs life events in my mind with the hope of achieving a particular or different outcome. This may apply to present, past, or future.

Belief in magic is found in presence. It is the willingness to see the wonder of life – powerful, beautiful, and not always pretty.

Faith supports my consciousness – with breathing, walking, eating, working. It recognizes and embraces the range of my emotional capacities and experiences. Faith allows me to notice and acknowledge. When faith combines with action, it enables me to live in right relationship to the world.

Magical thinking fosters unconscious and sub-conscious influences in my life. It clings to emotional reactions, damming their flow, and tripping up my emotional flexibility. When magical thinking combines with action, it disconnects me from myself and the world around me.

Belief in magic makes room for possibilities. It stimulates dreams and celebrates creativity. When belief in magic combines with action, it enables me to inspire and create change.

Faith listens and leans on prayer.

Magical thinking shuts its eyes, plugs its ears, and leans on wishes.

Belief in magic senses and leans on openness.

Faith knows the Sox will win the Series again, that the 836,000 pound airplane I board will ride on the wind, and that the surgeon's hand removed cancer from my left breast.

Magical thinking sees the Titanic in New York Harbor, the Twin Towers on the skyline, and Babe Ruth back in Boston.

Belief in magic leaves me awestruck in a field of fireflies, underneath the Northern Lights, and in the presence of people I love.

Faith is grounding and grounded in love. Faith supports and steadies me when I am hurt, challenged, grieving, or despairing. Faith offers a hope of greater meaning to life and life events.

Magical thinking is charming and sentimental. Magical thinking wants respite, rescue, and avoidance. Magical thinking wants to replace reality.

Belief in magic is inspiring and inspired by the boundlessness of love. Belief in magic recognizes the energies and forces that are with me day to day, which enrich my life, and offer comfort and perspective.

Trav'ler was the first puppy born into my hands. The chapters of our shared life spanned more than fifteen years. Her body was failing, falling. I was tempted by the whispers of magical thinking saying, "she will never die." Faith allowed me to let go of her companionship and her golden coat, where I buried my face and left my tears. Love had connected me with and devoted me to her essence. Faith assured me that her essence, her spirit, did not die. In an afternoon winter sky the sun shone through a break in the clouds, forming a golden shape – Trav'ler, young and smiling, running with front paws reaching for their next step. At home, I found this exact image of Trav'ler in my photo album. I believe. I believe in magic.

Living with honesty, in connection to my soul and its purpose is how I recognize what is alive in me – faith, magical thinking, belief in magic, something else, all of these, or none of these. I am tempted to label others' experiences, and then I am reminded that I do not dwell in their soul. I do not know the source of magic and universal power.

I just know they exist.

The Heart Finds Its Healing

In the three months leading to the 2016 Winter Solstice, Jess and I said final good-byes to three Chinooks who have contributed to the breed, had great character and soul, and were dearly loved.

Grieving was my heart's work that fall. The pack and I were in an extended state of adjustment – moving dog crates, serving up the correct number of meals, getting the right number of dog biscuits, knowing when all the dogs have entered the house, wondering who among the remaining dogs would assert alpha status.

My dogs knew something about building a community, nourishing hearts, and deepening relationships to the land. Healing has come through what they connected me with – being outside, living in the moment, listening more deeply, and loving.

Healing began before each death in the pure love that lives in caring for an aging, failing, and dying being. Every task rose above the mundane, becoming a sacred duty and an expression of love – cleaning up when they urinate or defecate inside; carrying them in and out of the house; hand feeding them; getting up with them in the night; sleeping on the sofa when they can't climb the stairs; stopping what I'm doing to stroke their coat and look into their eyes. This cultivated and nourished intuition, love, compassion, and gratitude for the aging and ailing one, for all of my dogs, for others in my life, and for myself.

September
Before she was taken for surgery on the day she died, I laid on the floor spooning with Redington. She was barely conscious. I put my hand in front of her nose. She smelled me, recognized me, and gently wagged her tail, resting her chin on my arm. In my fear, I whispered to her, "Please don't die." Knowing better, I immediately whispered again, "It's ok. It's ok if you have to go."

I kissed her muzzle, rubbed my face on her head, and nibbled on her ear. That was our goodbye.

November
A set of wind chimes hangs at the End of the Trail, where our dogs are laid to rest. We think of its chimes as the joy-filled, wagging tails of our dogs who have crossed the bridge. I brought Chocorua's body here to bury on the morning after her death. I listened for the chimes. They were silent. I laid Chocorua's body in the grave, placed an apple, her favorite treat, on her heart, tossed two handfuls of dirt, and spoke words of love. I sighed what words couldn't capture and buried my beloved dog. When the dirt at last covered her body, the wind chimes sounded reminding me to not look for Chocorua in her old body any more. She is free, running with the wind as she loved to do.

December
Charley died in the early morning hours on the day of the Winter Solstice. Later, I laid down to sleep with so much stirring in me. I dreamed I was viewing a tract of land from above, looking down at trees and fields. Across the field there was one solitary, tawny dog running free.

Sweet connections with my departed dogs continue to comfort and teach me – in savasana I re-experienced carrying Chocorua's lifeless body home – I felt her in my arms again. In a yoga posture I sensed puppies romping around my feet. Energy of my dogs arises in my home. Our spirits connect, transcending the boundaries of our physical forms.

Being a pack means loving and learning together, relating to one another's strengths and flaws, and living joyfully in the natural world. It is not perfection. And yet it is.

In this, the heart finds its healing.

A Trav'ler's Vow

I walk over meadow and woodland
Travel along roadways
Beside river, running free
A journey in which I carry
Not fear
No courage is needed
Only communion
Balance
With oak and acorn
I am welcomed home
Deer and coyote
Barred owl and field mouse
We greet one another
With love
In kinship
Mushroom and leaf
Trillium and lady slipper

Each footstep
Kisses earth
And marks
The center of the universe
It is not possible
For me to be lost

Nothing is mine
Only the treasure of
Infinite love

The earth holds me
Universe whispers
Inside my ear

My Father

My father, fox-like,
Observed this world
Allowed life to unfold
And made a difference
In his own way
With a humble man's touch
With a stealth love
And wisdom
Gained from learning
Across many lifetimes

Gone thirty years now
His presence remains in
Treasured dreams
Walking together through tall grass
In conversation
I don't remember our words
But oh, his presence lingers

I swear he lived again
As my beloved dog, Baxter
She sneezed like him
One after another
I would laugh and say
"Dad, is that you?"
My father's brown eyes
Would stare back at me

Today I am reminded
He is never far away
A heart connection
A tie that is never broken
A tie that tames my heart
When I am wary
And self-protective

Open now

I observe life
With gratitude
As life unfolds
And make a difference
In my own way

All is well

Dog Naps and Dreams

Dirigo rests her head on the brick hearth
She is still

Chocorua and Jack share the sofa –
Heads resting at either end, tails entwined
He lays on his side
Heaviness of his breath – a rhythmic humming
Soothing to me

Chocorua lays chin down
Silent breath and I pause
To watch for rise and fall
Along her body, reclined

I study the contours and colors of her face
Remembering the dog of 8 years ago
When we were still family
The puppy of 13 years ago
Who loved other dogs above all
And I wondered if she would give
A second thought to me

Love is a choice

You chose me or the idea of me quickly
When you really needed to choose yourself
The goodness of your being
Recognition of what brings you joy
Contentment
A fulfillment of your life's purpose

I loved being chosen
And loved you for your choice
And your goodness of being
When I really needed to choose myself

Chocorua raises her eyes from across the room
She holds my returning gaze
Jack whimpers at the far end of the couch

Four feet paddling
Dreaming of runs across fields
Through woods
Amidst his pack
Full on joyful dream
I am home

For Not Mowing

A young deer stepped out of the trees
An unmowed field between us
My dogs barked in alert
In curiosity

She was not afraid
But wise in the distance
She kept between

Two steps forward
Harvesting and eating
The greens in my field that
I decided I would not
Mow this year

Home

I am home
Restful
In no hurry
To be anywhere
But here
To do anything
But sit
Notice

Home
Sipping morning tea
From my old mug
Sitting at the oak desk
My grandfather made
Writing to you
Whoever you are

Chickadees
Finches
Pronounce
I am home
Dogs asleep at my feet
Know it
Dream it

Distant highway hums
Telling another's tale

Morning Meditation with Dogs

I sat in meditation
With six dogs
This morning
A Monday
And I desired
To walk wholehearted
Into the day
Before me

Tara Brach
Spoke softly
Through my iPhone
Instructing to
Relax the body
Relax the mind
Relax the heart

I breathe in deeply
To my belly
And out slowly with a
Dog's sigh
Ease in the withers
Paws lay effortlessly
Microadjustments
Bring comfort
In each resting spot

Deep breath in
Groaning
Release
Exhale a sigh

And I walk
Wholehearted
Into the day

My Teachers

My dogs don't know
Classic yoga poses
They do know that
When I stretch down
To reach the earth
That it is called
Downward, Dog!
They say onward dog
And rush to share kisses
With my exhale

I focus on the moment
And joy wags in my heart

A Blank Page

When I concentrate on this
Blank page
That is exactly
What I get

Earth speaks though...
And my heart replies

My old dog
Sleeping next to me
On the sofa
Tells me a story...
I nod

The stones on the woodstove
Sigh and remind me
Of greater truths
Of simpler truths...
I bow

A page transforms
I transform
With...
Wisdom
Love
Creation

Mother Remembering

He arrived like that
My child
He was 16 years old
New to me
Whole and beautiful and complete
We learned about each other
I got to love him
Care for him
Show him how I got back up
After making mistakes
Experiencing losses
Falling

We laughed a lot
Healing
Growing in trust and love

He arrived a cat person
And left for college with dog fur over all his stuff

Eighteen years later
We facetimed last night
Hanging out with each other across the miles
While he prepared his dinner
While I paused at the end of my day
At the end of a few months of
Losses, mistakes, falling down

I always thought that mothers
Instantly love the children they give birth to
Having been closer than close
Through pregnancy and delivery
Maybe this is so

I remember the instant I loved Braden
Such a sweet moment to remember

1:30 AM

You wag at the foot of my bed
Thump, thump, thump
1:30 am
My light is on
I lie awake
Thinking of the Iranian
Stranded at the airport
The Syrian
Not even allowed to board her flight

The world watches
Wonders
Remembers
The crowds jeer and cheer
"This is what democracy looks like"
Bannon has a place on the NSC

My friend – Muslim
With a green card
US wife
Three children born here
Kind, devoted, loving
Contributes to his community
Has a beautiful smile
Lives his values
And is bizarrely in contrast
To the pussy-grabbing
Commander-in-thief
Whose executive disorders
Defy who we think we are
This xenophobic, narcissistic
Puppet-of-his-ego
Puppet-of-white-nationalists
Short-timer
Unleashes a torrent
Against the planet

Humanity, core values
He will be fired
He will be called history's despicable

McConnell, shriveled and counting his change,
And his ilk
Cower in the shadows

There It Is

Jackman sleeps on the sofa
With eyes open
Not for the need of trust
It is for the need of connection
He relaxes in rest
Yet his sleepy brain registers
Glimpses of the one he loves
This is his everyday
His paw drapes off the sofa
His blocky brown head
Propped on the diminutive Dirigo
Curled up next to him

I sit in my rocker across the room
The woodstove creaks and pops
Warming my left side
Jackman's breathing is long
And steady
I listen and try to match his breath
He raises an eyebrow
In approval I think to myself
The sun opens one eye
And closes it again
Pulling the covers up over its head
As snow falls on this February morning
"Just ten more minutes" the sun appeals

And so it is
This is my everyday
So routine that I might not see it
Sometimes I do not see it
    When I have a grant to write
    A woman to cry over
    A resistance to keep up with

But there it is
Everyday

>What we are defiantly defending
>What we are longing to share
>What we are working to care for

Connection
There it is

Life, Death, and Wonder

What has died
Lives on
Hope is born on this day
And tattoos my heart
With love eternal

But Today

At a younger age
Baring would have bit
This young upstart
At least growled
And snapped
He did not possess
Tolerance
For other dogs
Who entered his space

But today
At fifteen
He ambles over to an
Occupied dog bed
He curls his body against
The bigger boy-dog
Six years his junior
Allows this youngster to
Hold him down
And wash his only exposed ear
Even
For longer
Than feels good

One
Acting in devotion
Giving, nurturing, grooming
One
Allowing
Receiving care and cleansing

Tied to Generations

Tied to generations and
Relations with tales to tell
Among moments
That will never become recorded history
Victorious as a peacekeeper who
Loves with no sentimentality –
Just pure love
Earthy and knowing
She walks through this world
Recognizing only what is real

Life, Death and Wonder with a Pack of Dogs
At the passing of Hurricane Baring Downeast
March 15, 2001 – November 5, 2015

At the time of this writing, it is nearly 3 days since Hurricane Baring Downeast (aka Baring or "Buddy") died. Though nearly 15 years old, his decline and dying was fast and abrupt upon my return home from a work road trip. I took him to the vets on Thursday night seeking treatment for symptoms that he was exhibiting. I never expected that I would come home alone.

As I described Baring's symptoms in the past few days with my vet I watched Baring lying on the exam table, I began to see his surrender. I called Jess, who co-owns Baring. We talked through what was happening and she supported my decision. It was time to say good-bye. Jess sat in meditation in her home as Baring was euthanized, holding both of us in loving compassion. She burned juniper for Baring, wishing him love and peace. When the last of the juniper burnt out, she received a text from me that he was gone. His passing was peaceful. I hope that I am as ready and calm when my time comes.

I returned home Thursday evening – alone, tired, and sad. I wondered if and hoped that my dogs would smell the story of his dying on me. I held Baring as he died, my face and tears buried in his fur, his last breaths touched my forehead. My hand rested on his chest, feeling his heartbeat slowly fade then stop. All the dogs sniffed me and yet I can't tell you what they smelled. I just wanted them to know.

At bedtime Otter settled in her blue crate – across from the empty crate where Baring had slept. I climbed the stairs to my room, noticing she would be alone downstairs, where she preferred to sleep. I wondered if and how that would change in time.

I left the next morning for a work retreat and returned on midday Saturday, leaving the dogs in the care of my longtime dogsitter. My vet had held Baring's body until my return, so that he could be buried in the dog's resting place here at the farm – the spot we call "The End of the Trail." Jess picked up Baring's body and met me at the farm.

We brought him to the dog yard, laying him on the grass and brought all the dogs out to see him. One by one they recognized his presence, cautiously and curiously sniffing his body, his head. The very last to notice him was Otter. We lingered as the dogs circled us, greeting Jess and then returning to smell Baring, allowing them to figure it out – to integrate what this change would mean for the pack. After a few minutes had passed, they were done with their investigation of his lifeless body. Baring was no longer there.

We buried his body at The End of the Trail. He lies next to WoodsRunner Allagash who died shortly after we moved to the farm. The great mountain looks down upon where his body rests. Jess found a stone to mark his grave. It bears an uncanny resemblance to Baring's profile – his sloping stop, his silky down ears, his darkened and blocky muzzle. We stood at his gravesite and told stories with smiles and misty eyes; stories of his sweetness, his silliness, how handsome he was, and his stubborn habits.

That evening I enjoyed a quiet dinner at my friends' house, telling the same stories – of Baring's last day and memorable moments of my life with him. At some point the conversation turned to our work, politics, and house projects. Life moves on. I returned home weary and ready for sleep. I started the bedtime routine with the dogs, ushering them outside for the last potty call, then bringing them in to find their beds – each dog dashing to the same spot they'd been sleeping in for years, some for their lifetimes. Except…Otter. I brought the bedtime dog biscuit to Otter and she was not in her blue crate, but instead she stood in Baring's crate, awaiting her treat. I smiled and said, "yes."

I woke at 6:30 this morning – Sunday, a day of rest. Rising with my six dogs, I passed a window and saw the sun just above the great mountain's horizon. It has been in sunrises where I "see"

Trav'ler since she died in January. I smiled this morning, wondering if Baring lingers in the sunrise with her, wondering where will I "see" him in my days.

I prepared breakfast for the dogs – a routine practice of how much food, who is served in what order and where each dog eats. My dogs stand ready for this predictable pattern. Jackman gets his food in a crate just because he is so rambunctious and excited to eat. Chocorua and Dirigo receive their food next, eating near the counter and the cookbooks. Otter is then served on the rug that runs through the hallway near the back door. Redington and Charley are served by the stove.

This morning Otter, sniffed her food and walked away. This was very unusual for her and reminded me of Baring's breakfast routine over the past months. He was slow to start his breakfast – many times walking away from his food. I'd pick up his food and serve him later, after I'd shepherded the dogs who had already eaten out to the yard. I'd suspected that he liked being alone in the house with his breakfast. I came to enjoy these quiet moments with him.

On this morning, I picked up Otter's food dish and offered it to her again. She walked away – across the kitchen past the other dogs to the spot where Baring ate – next to the water dish. She looked up at me as if requesting that I serve her there. A bit stunned, I set her food down and she put her muzzle into her dish and ate her food without looking up again – it was the Otter I am used to seeing with food.

Except…she stands on the vinyl floor eating her food, relaxed as can be. You see, Otter is the primary reason there are throw rugs throughout the first floor, covering the slippery floor. She has stood, crying and frozen, seeing an expanse of flooring ahead of her – between her and entering or exiting the house. She is the reason there's a little rug at each door, a long runner in the back hallway, a throw rug in the kitchen and one in the middle of the living room. She steels herself as she moves from rug to rug, steadying her footing as she leaves one "safety zone" and passes to another rug.

Not this morning. She stood soundly, eating in a spot where before she would have never dreamed of eating. Her feet calmly planted where her father's feet stood for meal after meal.

I suspect there are many places and moments in which I will know Baring is present. On this morning, I know he lives on in his daughter.

Haikus

For Baring

Earthly light darkened
A new star rose to the sky
In space, love lives on

For Chocorua

She would overturn
All dog dishes to find more
Post breakfast silence

The Whelping

Nesting as we wait
Digging and biting – we watch
Whining for new life

For Trav'ler

Trav'ler rises to
Remind us that love lives on
Shining, glorious

Solstice Birth

The fiery glory of the Northern Lights
Emblazoned the late summer sky with a vision
A foretelling – announcing the arrival of the ones to come
And commanding the northern wind
To carry this news far beyond

"Honor has been bestowed to those who were due
The one standing in judgment has created new life
Let it be known that magic has been done
And peace remains
Soldiers, lay down your arms
Seafaring warriors, turn away from battle
Return home
Make ready for the ones to come"

And so it was a year of change and transition
A moving of many –
Carrying forward the lives lived before
Facing uncertain opportunities ahead on new paths
Choices would be made with the wisdom of generations
To create readiness for the ones to come

Then came the Solstice of that year
And the birth of Ull, Riahannon, Aske and Aquilo
On an island which links all time
The four brought blessings
To the hands that cradled their arrival
And to the mother who labored and delivered and loved

Under the glow of the new moon
They brought gifts to their kind,
Sending pure white snow to their grandmother –
The trav'ler in the north
Delivering joy to the great mountain, across the land
Inspiring hope that others may follow where they lead

Old Dog

The old dog lies heavily at my side
Heaving chest with deep and steady
Breathing – like a lullaby
Soothing and hypnotic

Twitching feet
Lumber through today's dreams
Replacing those of old –
      Chasing rabbits
      Bearing a sled's weight
      Across snowy and wooded trails

Today's dreams are simpler
      My hands across her fur
      A slow and satisfying walk
      Following me on my heel

I stay frozen in this moment
Thick fur rising and falling
White eyelashes clasped together
Four paws intertwined
As if in prayer

My Favorite Dreams

I have favorite dreams in my lifetime. Not a lot, maybe five or six. They are dreams that seem more like a magical transmission or communication with the divine in the deep of the night.

After my father died, he came to me in a dream. We walked on the beach, through tall dune grass and talked. Nothing that was said was memorable. It was simply being in his company again that I hold as a precious memory.

In another dream, I shared conversation and an ice cream sandwich with Abraham Lincoln.

After Charley and Chocorua died, I had vivid dreams about each of them. I could feel Chocorua in my arms as I carried her home after she died. I could see Charley running free in an open field, running to the end of the trail.

These dreams so connected with life realities, emerged from a heart moved by what I knew of this world and what I yearned for.

One particularly beautiful dream took place on the streets of Portland many years ago. At the time, I lived in a neighboring town. In my dream I was standing on Washington Avenue in Portland where the exit ramp ends just below the Eastern Promenade. I had the startling recognition that I was supposed to be home momentarily. On foot and without a car, I knew I wouldn't make it there on time. I pondered for a moment. But for just a moment.

Then, as if it were a commonplace solution, I lowered myself until I was on my hands and knees. My vision focused on my hands, on the ground in front on me. I watched them as my hands turned into the unmistakably big snowshoe paws that belonged to my dog, Cheena. Her fur and skin traveled up my wrists and arms as I watched myself transform into her.

Cheena was a brawny female with heavy bones, a broad chest, and a strong, athletic body. Cheena's early life was one of disappointment, longing, and confinement. She came into my life when she was five, with anxiety and fears that built up in her over those early years. She was awkwardly sweet, innocent, and loving. Any guest who visited wanted to bring her home.

One of my joys was watching her run – both for the grace, beauty, and speed she achieved, and for the serenity that became visible in this otherwise anxious dog. It was breathtaking to watch her run.

The transformation from my human body to her athletic dog body completed. In my dream, I was not watching her run. I was her – running. I watched, not from afar, but from inside of her. I ran through the streets of Portland toward Westbrook seeing and experiencing speed, agility, and strength from her dogs-eye view. It was as if she shared it with me.

What took my breath away from all my prior observations of her running, became part of my breathing as her running.

I don't recall getting home in that dream. That was not the point. As in life, it's not the destination, but the journey.

Trav'ler on a Rainy Spring Day

I see Cheena in your eyes
These days
Wide and wondering
With hints of worry and want
That marked her days
After they were built in her
During those five years

Early and open
We are
Absorbing definitions
From our environment
And our hearts' relation
To it

The universe gives us breath
And a loving soul
To tend our beating heart
    Our feeling heart
        Our breaking heart
And slow the traffic
In our minds

My heart opens and wells for you
And Cheena, gone a decade

You trust the certainty in
My returning gaze
Trust that was built from the beginning
And nurtured these 15 years

I see Cheena in your eyes
These days
I breathe with you
And all is well

The Story

Young dogs
Inhabit spots on the sofa
One – two – three
Dirigo – Jackman – Redington
Heads propped against
Arms and each other
Tawny paws draped over cushions
Lingering in space

The old ones
Trav'ler – Chocorua – Otter
Sprawl across dog beds
Upon throw rugs
Safely held in the pull of gravity
Deep sighs
Steady breath
Beings
Present for another day

I disappear
Into my mind
Seeking to know
And understand
The story
Which holds us all
Ancient and unchanging

For Trav'ler, Who Lives On

I turned to my dear friend
And said
"I thought she would never die"

I kissed you on your forehead
Then I said good-bye

Now I see you in the sunrise
In light and anticipation
Of each new day
Present and steadfast

I feel you in the
Aches and rhythm
In my heart
My heart –
Magnified
Wiser
Broken open
From life and death
With you

I hold you in my memories
Your face
Your deep brown eyes
Your movement among others
Across snowy fields
Images of you
Cataloged like old photographs
Carefully organized in albums
Or tucked away – nearly forgotten
And marking my place
In the book of my life
I turn a page
There you are

You move with each footstep
My inhale and exhale
You are nestled in
The misty pockets of my eyes
The upturned corners of my mouth
Your smile on my face

We are not merged
I am who I am
Because we have been
In relation to one another
To the sun and the moon
The rain and earth

You are alive in me
I am nourished by the love that remains
Only to harvest more love

To carry this gift from you
Means I also carry the duty
To feed a hungry world

And you live on

What is Born?

What is born
During this cold time
When many
And much has died
Leaving my flesh tattooed with grief

I stare down the fierce
And northern wind
Cold to my bones
I'll be damned if I show
A shiver

I wrap myself in my warmest coat
Three dogs burst ahead of me
We take to the wooded trails
To find what is born

Ladyslipper and trillium
Fast asleep
Dreaming of days in May
The swimming hole
Frozen over with ice
Chickadee and jays
Dance in the sky
No eggs to lay

Pale blue sky is born
Sun has risen
A promise made and fulfilled each day
Cedar and pine
Stand in strength
Dogs run ahead on the trail
Then circle back
To be at my side
Over and over again
Devotion born each time

   We ascend the mountain trail

Stepping over ice and birch logs
And stones
History keepers
With tales to tell of
Time gone by
And what is new
On this day

We stand on an
Outcropping of rock
Against the wind
With each other
To see the world before us
Mount Washington and Chocorua
On the far horizon

I close my eyes
Open them again
For I thought I saw
One lone tawny dog
Run across the field below
Toward the end of the trail

I shiver
What has died
Lives on
Hope is born on this day
And tattoos my heart
With love eternal

Fly Free
(For Ande)

How often
Do we witness
The last breath
Of one we love?
The moment before
All love
Infinity

The last breath
Last touch
One last look
Into deep brown eyes

So we learn
How to love
With a steady heart
Open hands
Our feet firmly
On the ground
As we bid the
One we love to
Fly free among the stars
Among those we have loved
Fly free
Assured that
We will meet again

Who Will Be the Alpha Dog?

Just weeks after Charley died, I sent this text message to Jess:
Question of the day.
Who would you wish for as alpha dog?
Otter?
Jack?
Dirigo?
It's like the three stooges.

The text message I got in response from Jess was just one word:
You!

She was right.

I grieved for Red, Chocorua and Charley. And for Baring and Trav'ler who died the year prior. They were giants, big personalities, wise and amazing dogs in so many ways. Otter, Jack and Dirigo are sweet and silly goof balls. I thought I was funny when I referred to them as Larry, Curly, and Moe.

It had been nearly 20 years since I lived with so few dogs. At first all I noticed was what was missing – at mealtime and bedtime, going for walks, the start of the day, and the end of the day. I kept bumping into the empty spaces where they resided in our day to day life together. I felt grief and sadness.

And then I began to notice what was there. I turned to the trio of dogs who remained – Otter, Jackman, and Dirigo. I noticed I had received a gift – attention, touch, time, energy that could be distributed in greater quantities to 3 dogs rather than 6 or 8 or 13.

Life with a pack of 13 dogs had been full and busy and adventurous. Though not the most well-mannered or well trained dogs, all of my them had their own character, so memorable and devoted. Moxie insisted that a human constantly touch her – she insisted - constantly. Jackman leapt up for hugs – especially when you weren't looking. Rangeley ate eyeglasses, television remotes and cookbooks. Baring picked on puppies. Cheena ate through dog sled lines. Trav'ler had a penchant for eating sticks of butter. Or chicken. Or cheesecake. I awoke one morning and came down the stairs to make coffee and feed the dogs. It was quiet and serene. Trav'ler was curled up in a ball, sleeping soundly – on the dining room table.

A pack of three. There is an opportunity here – even with Larry, Curly, and Moe. I watched my routines and observed the habits I had developed in order to manage a pack. I now could choose new routines, new ways of being. I added moments of dog training throughout our daily routine. Dirigo, age 5, learned sit, stay, wait, watch me, and heel – all in the space of time after she finished each meal – while Otter and Jackman were still eating. Jackman, age 11, learned to keep his butt on the ground – no small feat. Otter, age 13, learned to watch me – and that was enough. The mini training sessions showed benefits on our free runs in the woods. Dirigo responded more quickly to my recall because she had been learning that good things happen when she is responsive. Now there's a life lesson.

With more of my attention on them, I began to see more of their character. Silly dogs? Why yes. They are also loving, devoted, and energetically connected to life. I engaged more with Jackman and his poet's soul. I spent more time cuddling with Dirigo. I figured out the optimal throw rug combinations to make life less stressful for Otter, who was terrified of the vinyl floors. Jackman and Dirigo became more playful with one another – Jack, at age 11, played like a young puppy.

I felt joy. And my heart commenced mending.

In mid-January, someone broke into my garage while I slept. In the end nothing was stolen, except for my sense of safety and ease. Well, that wasn't stolen either, but I felt uncomfortable and more fearful living alone. I made efforts to create more home security, including having the dogs no longer sleeping in crates during the night. Dirigo was a wonderful snuggle dog. Jackman, though, needed to remind me 2 or 3 times a night that he was still there and that he still loved me. All in all it was worth it to be surrounded by my guardians (yes, Larry, Curly, and Moe). Still, I wondered what in the world they would do if faced with an intruder.

We were establishing a new normal. My heart was mending.

We walked in the woods every weekend, sometimes with friends. In early March, we walked over the hard packed and icy trails. The anticipation of spring was alive in me, but boy this day was bitter cold. It was nice to get into the wooded trails and out of the wind. We walked together. The dogs would run off to explore and circle back to be by my side, then off they would go again. Over and over. It was perfect. We turned onto the trail that has no name, the one that winds and rises and falls through the trees. Around one bend, I heard a rustle in the woods and thought "oh, a deer." I turned and saw a man walking in the woods just yards away from me. In my woods. I felt fright that pushed me back a step. I didn't make a sound until the dogs charged in his direction, barking. I called to them. They stood shoulder to shoulder holding a perimeter between me and this "intruder" in my woods. They barked. They stood in silence. They did not wag. They did not take their eyes off him.

There's not much more of a story about the man in the woods – he just walked away without saying a word. The real story is about the dogs, my companions, who knew exactly what to do. They were not the Three Stooges. They were my super-heroes – knowing, wise and strong.

A Sunday Walk in the Woods

A December Sunday
Walking with Ira
And five Chinooks
Across fields turned hard
From nights in the twenties
And days that are finally seasonably cold
The icy wind blows
And we look forward
To the shelter of wooded trails
Through a well-marked
Opening between oak and birch

Traversing familiar ground
Where dog sled runners
Have passed in near silence
Where paw prints and foot prints remain
Like kisses with fresh lipstick
On earth's inflexible face

On the trail that has no name
One-two-three-four-five dogs
Dart and dash about
Counting is like breath in
Breath out
They run ahead and
Circle back
At our request – for a treat
And of their own accord
Greeted upon return
With a touch and cheer

Do body memories rise in them
On these trails
As they do in me?
Does their imagination fly
As they fly
Around pines

Over rocks and ice?
Is their thinking concrete
Present only to this moment
And to what is - right now?

Do they feel the same wonder as I?

First Fire

First morning
Broken clouds
Gray and pink and blue
Silence but for
Breath
Heartbeat
Stirring life
Crackling and humming of the
First fire
Gold and green and blue
Greeting this day
Welcoming this year

I thought you'd
Want to know that
Last January
I took a teaspoon
Of Trav'ler's remains –
The dust her body had become
When spirit and breath had left her
I added them to
The canning jar filled with
Ashes from the first fire of
The last year

As I do
I held them in my hands
Clasped in prayerful listening
Returned them to the fire
Connecting time
Memories
Dreams
Gratitude and grief

Acknowledging
The path and we are one

Celebration
*This poem is written in honor and recognition
of the 100th anniversary of the first Chinook's birth.*

We gather in celebration
As they did a century ago
Ningo missed the sledding season
1917 – in New Hampshire's wintry chill
Waiting, waiting
Not knowing what was to come

Snowshoe paws impressed upon
The Intervale's whitened tundra
They arrived with an ear for learning
Eager to please
Smart, stubborn, sturdy
Accomplished on trail and hearth
Celebrated in headlines
And in solemn moments held by human hearts
To the very end of the earth

We gather in celebration
Of what was born
On Wonalancet Farm
One hundred years ago
Chimes arise from our bell tower
Across distance and time
People will know
That we stand together to
Remember and bless
Those who came before
Those who promised us that
We would always remember
Let us hold in reverence
And speak the names
Of those we've loved and lost

We gather in celebration
Of their kin
Who abide with us on this day
Strong and enduring
Beauty and grace
Let love well our hearts
As we speak their names
To one another

We cannot see what is to come
So we love this moment
Standing at the center of it all
Offering honor to whom honor is due
To the very end of the trail

About the Author

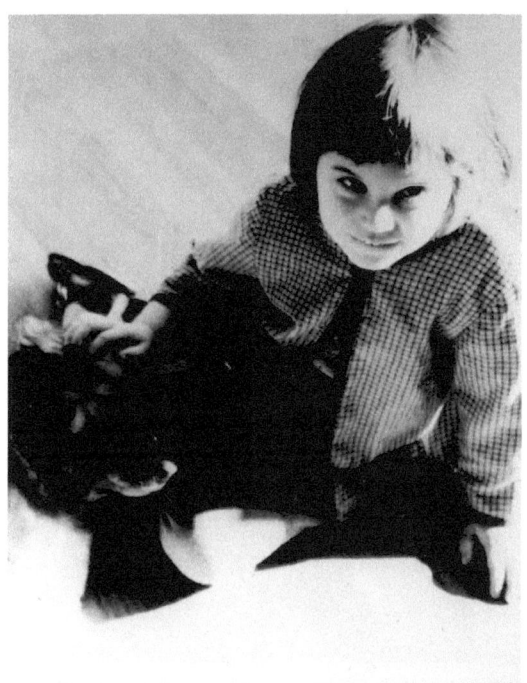

Penthea Burns lives on a farm in rural Maine. This farm has produced Christmas trees, herbs, vegetables, and berries. And Chinook dogs. And ideas. And love. And poetry.

A life in Maine suits her. Her roots and purpose are here. By day, Penthea is a senior policy associate at a local university and a community organizer – promoting capacity building, justice, and love. Her visits with her son and her family keep her connected with what's most important. She enjoys the companionship of her dogs, dear friends, good movies, or a good book. She is a student of compassionate communication and decolonization in order to make a contribution to life.

In the early morning hours, with heart, brain and gut in communion, Penthea sits by the woodstove and writes poetry.

She loves her life and she is glad to share it.

More Poetry by Penthea Burns

**My Prognosis:
I Live**

My Prognosis: I Live

"Inspirational and moving poetry arising out of the personal journey of one woman finding peace and strength from her environment. It reminds us again of how the simplest things can move us forward or hold out the stillness that feeds us. Offered as a gift of love to the reader, this slim volume speaks to the age-old truth that healing comes from within, and from one another. Cover photos are from Great Mountain Farm in Maine, and depict two of the author's daily paths with her beloved dogs. Read these poems and take heart."

~ Pat Malcolm

"Warm and compelling, My Prognosis: I Live invites the reader to Live in the moment and take in everything around you. There is a comfortable, positive, calm in each poem that is personal to the author – yet relatable and rewarding to the reader."

~ Lynn Price